Santa's
Magic
Candy Cane

Written by Michael Stringer

Illustrations by Wathmi de Zoysa

Santa's
Magic
Candy Cane

Fat Dog Books
ISBN: 978-0-9991370-9-3
Fiction/Children's Stories

Printed in the United States of America

Visit our website at www.fatdogbooks.com

For my daughters,
Cadence and Emma,
who inspired this fable through
their love of children's books,
my bedtime stories, and the
holidays. And for my wife,
Laura, who loves Christmas
more than anyone I know.

Bailey's favorite time of the year is Christmas. She loves the tree decorated with shiny ornaments, and watching Daddy hang lights around the house. Mommy bakes her yummy gingerbread cookies and delicious apple crumb pies. And the house always smells sweet like a bakery.

More than anything in the world, Bailey loves
Santa Claus. As a curious little girl, Bailey dreamed
up new questions about Santa all the time.
"Why does Santa deliver presents to all the boys and
girls?" Bailey asked.
"Because he wants all the boys and girls to be happy
on Christmas day," Mommy said.
"How many Reindeer does Santa have for his sleigh?"
"Santa has nine Reindeer, and Rudolph
leads them all," Daddy said.
"How does Santa get into all the houses?"
"He comes down the chimney, of course," Daddy said.
Yes, she thought, Daddy is right.

Every Christmas morning, Bailey finds the cookies
she put out for Santa have been gobbled up and the
glass of milk nearly empty. And without fail, there's
a stack of presents underneath the tree.
One chilly day while playing with her toys, Bailey
suddenly stopped and looked around. Her family
moved to this new house months ago, but something
was missing. The living room in this house had no
fireplace. Bailey thought, how could this be?
How could Santa bring all those presents into a
house with no chimney to climb down?

At bedtime, Bailey kept thinking about the mystery of the house with no chimney. She looked at her bedroom window, but knew her parents kept the windows closed tightly during the winter. It was far too freezing cold to leave them open. They would each turn into a snowman! Bailey tried to imagine how Santa could sneak inside without an unlocked door or window. She knew Daddy locked the front door every night before bedtime. She could not stop worrying that Santa would have to skip her new house on Christmas Eve.

Late into the snowy evening, Bailey finally
fell into a deep slumber. She began to dream
something so amazing that when she woke
up, her eyes popped wide open. Bailey jumped
out of bed and ran into her parents' bedroom.
"Wake up, wake up!" Bailey shouted.
"Bailey, what is it?" Daddy said
in his sleepy voice.
"I know! I know how he gets in!"
"Who honey, how who gets in?" Mommy said.
"Santa! I know how Santa gets into a house
with no chimney!"
"You do?" Mommy said.

"I saw it in my dream. Santa has this big candy cane with red and green stripes, and it looks see-through, like a glass cup! He hangs the candy cane over the doorknob and it lights up like Rudolph's nose!"
"Then what happens?" Mommy asked.
"The door swings open, like magic!"
Daddy agreed, "That's right, Bailey. Nothing can stop Santa from delivering his toys to children."

Bailey couldn't believe her good luck, to dream about Santa's magic candy cane. She spent most of the day drawing pictures of the candy cane, trying to match the one she saw in her dream. Just a few days later, it was Christmas Eve. Bailey put a plate with three cookies and a tall glass of milk on the coffee table. She no longer felt worried about Santa skipping her house, and just moments after Daddy tucked her snugly into bed, Bailey fell asleep.

For Santa

When she awoke the next morning, Bailey knew it was Christmas! She was so excited she almost didn't notice a present at the end of her bed. It was about the size of a shoebox, wrapped in a big, red bow. Bailey crawled out from underneath her covers to get a closer look. The outside of the box sparkled with colors of bright gold, red and green. There was even a red and white sticker on the box with words. "Fr...om... the..." Bailey slowly sounded out the words, "Nor...th... Po...le." Oh my goodness, she thought. What could possibly be inside this fancy box from the North Pole?

Bailey gently carried the box into the living room,
where Mommy and Daddy were enjoying a cup of hot
chocolate on the sofa.
"Mommy, Daddy, look what I found!" Bailey shouted.
"What's this?" Daddy asked.
"A present from the North Pole!"
"The North Pole! That's wonderful,
open it up," Mommy said.

Before she did, Bailey noticed the cookies were gone and the glass of milk was empty. And under the tree, sure enough, she could see a bunch of brightly wrapped presents. Santa came to her house!

Bailey untied the red bow and took off the lid. Inside, she found several layers of thin, white tissue paper, folded neatly and held together by a silver ribbon. Her heart was pounding and her skin got goosebumps.

Bailey undid the silver ribbon, peeled back the tissue paper and found a large, glass candy cane, just like the one in her dream! It was beautiful! It was shiny! It was unbelievable! Bailey carefully lifted the candy cane, her eyes growing bigger with excitement.

"Wow, look at that!" Daddy said.
Bailey also noticed a greeting card, folded in half
at the bottom of the box. On the front cover
was a photo of Santa.
"Mommy, please read it to me, hurry!" Bailey said,
handing Mommy the card.

Dear Bailey,

Merry Christmas! You are holding something very
special in your hands, Santa's Magic Candy Cane.
I give them to children like you who believe in
the goodness of Santa. May this Magic Candy Cane
always remind you of Santa and fill your heart
with the spirit of Christmas!

Santa Claus

"Santa gave me a Magic Candy Cane!" Bailey
shouted with glee. "This is the
best Christmas ever!!!"